TALES FROM AMERICANA

Johnny Appleseed

BY MARLEY RICHMOND

Kids Core

An Imprint of Abdo Publishing
abdobooks.com

Disney made a short film about Johnny Appleseed in 1948.

CHAPTER 1

Planting Seeds

A young man stepped through tall grass. His eyes searched the land. His feet were bare. As a shirt, he wore a coffee sack with holes cut out for his arms. He was wearing a tin pan as a hat.

Johnny Appleseed walked through parts of the United States planting apple seeds.

The man was Johnny Appleseed. He was looking for a place to plant apple trees.

Johnny found a spot. He began to plant apple seeds. He pulled them from the leather sack he always carried. After burying the seeds, Johnny looked for fallen trees nearby. He used them to create a fence around the seeds. He didn't want deer or bears to eat the apple trees when they began to grow. Johnny thought that a family might want to settle nearby. Once the trees were bigger, they would provide apples for the family.

No Shoes?

Most stories about Johnny Appleseed say that he rarely wore shoes. In one story, a man gave Johnny a pair of old shoes. But later, Johnny was still barefoot. He had met a woman who needed them more than he did. He gave her the shoes.

This illustration of Johnny Appleseed dates back to the 1860s.

Johnny settled in for the night. He prepared to sleep under the stars. When the evening turned cold, he built a fire. The fire was nice and warm. But Johnny noticed something. Mosquitoes hovered near the flames. They were being burned! He got some water and put out the fire. Johnny wouldn't hurt another creature for his own comfort.

A Man and a Myth

Stories about Johnny Appleseed talk about a **generous** man who cared for nature. He lived in harmony with everyone he met. He walked across parts of the United States, planting apple seeds as he went.

Johnny Appleseed helped plant apple trees as far west as present-day Indiana.

But Johnny Appleseed was a real man named John Chapman. He lived from 1774 to 1845. These were the early days of the United States. **Settlers** began to move north of the

Ohio River. Much of this land was taken from American Indians. When the United States claimed the land, it was named the Northwest Territory. Chapman traveled through this territory and planted apple seeds. Later in his life, Chapman became known as Johnny Appleseed. Although he has become a **legend**, many stories about his life hold some truth.

Explore Online

Visit the website below. What new information did you learn about Johnny Appleseed that wasn't in Chapter One?

The Story of Johnny Appleseed

abdocorelibrary.com/johnny-appleseed

John Chapman sometimes showed settlers how to plant apple seeds.

CHAPTER 2

John Chapman

People know only a few details about Chapman's early life. He was born on September 26, 1774, in Leominster, Massachusetts. His mother died before he was two years old. Chapman's father later married another woman.

This painting is considered to be one of the most realistic depictions of John Chapman.

In total, Chapman had 12 siblings. He left home when he was about 18 years old.

Chapman followed the religious teachings of a Christian named Emanuel Swedenborg. Swedenborg believed all living beings should be treated with respect. As he traveled, Chapman preached this belief and others. He often read the Bible aloud to settlers.

The Seeds of America

In the 1790s, the US Congress wanted more people to move into the Northwest Territory and develop the land. Congress donated the land to a company. The company would give families 100 acres (40 ha) of land to develop. Families had to plant 50 apple trees on their land to prove that they would stay.

Chapman traveled through the Northwest Territory. He planted apple seeds to start the **orchards** that settlers would need. He would sell the young trees to settlers. When people could not afford his trees, Chapman sometimes gave them away for free.

The seeds Chapman planted grew a bitter type of apple. People didn't eat these apples.

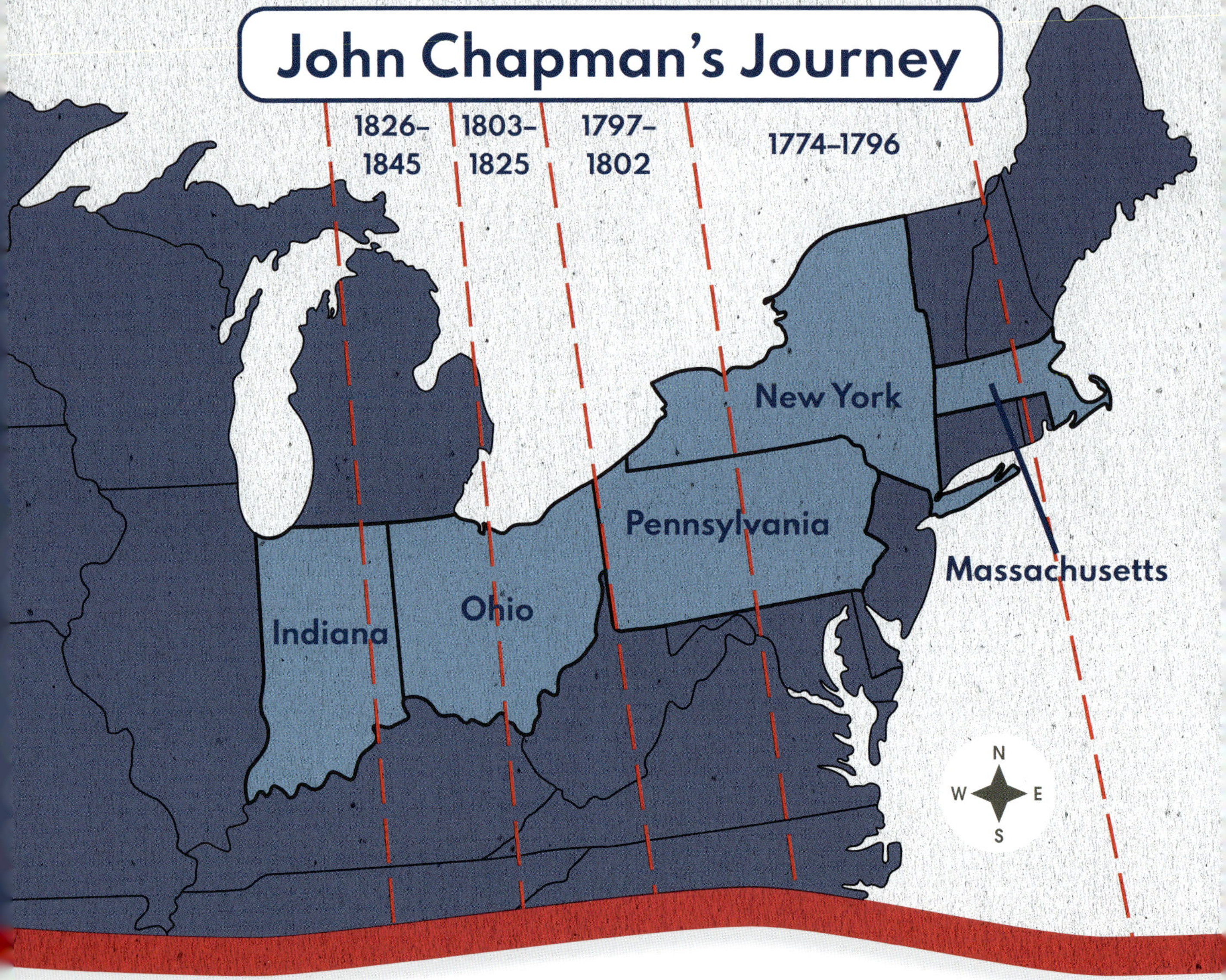

John Chapman planted apple seeds across five US states. The map above shows where he traveled during certain years. He began his journey in Massachusetts. He died in Indiana in 1845.

The fruit was made into hard apple cider. At that time, it was difficult to find clean drinking water. **Bacteria** in dirty water can make people sick.

But bacteria can't grow in hard apple cider. So settlers drank that instead.

Becoming Johnny Appleseed

Chapman traveled on foot for more than 50 years. He usually slept outside. He made friends with many people during his journey.

Planting an Apple Tree

Most apple trees are grown through a process called grafting. This is when part of a living apple tree is inserted into the stem of a young tree. The inserted part continues growing. Grafting is the best way to grow delicious apples. But Chapman thought grafting hurt trees. So he planted seeds instead.

Johnny Appleseed is often shown wearing worn-out clothing. Stories say that he would give better-quality clothes to people in need.

Settlers shared stories about the kind man who traveled through their towns and planted apple trees. Late in his life, Chapman was given the nickname Johnny Appleseed.

Chapman died in 1845. But the legend of Johnny Appleseed lived on. Chapman planted trees on more than 1,200 acres (486 ha) of land across the Northwest Territory. For years to come, people told stories and wrote poems about Johnny Appleseed.

Primary Source

One poem about Johnny Appleseed was written by Rosemary Carr Bénet and Stephen Vincent Bénet. They wrote:

> Of Jonathan Chapman
> Two things are known,
> That he loved apples,
> That he walked alone.

Source: Rosemary Bénet and Stephen Vincent Bénet. "Johnny Appleseed." *Your Daily Poem*, n.d., yourdailypoem.com. Accessed 17 Apr. 2023.

Comparing Texts

Think about the poem. Does it support the information in this chapter? Or does it give a different perspective? Explain how in a few sentences.

Apples are the most popular fruit in the United States. Most apples are eaten fresh, but they can also be used to make cider, juice, and applesauce.

CHAPTER 3

Johnny Appleseed Today

Chapman's apple trees lived long after he died. But in the 1920s, most of them were chopped down. The Prohibition Era began in 1920. Alcohol, including hard apple cider, was illegal during this time. Only a few of Chapman's trees survived.

John Henschel works at Weaver's Orchard in Pennsylvania. He dresses as Johnny Appleseed on Johnny Appleseed Day.

Some people believe that one of the trees Chapman planted lived into the 2000s. People have used branches from Chapman's original trees to grow new ones. These branches can be inserted into the stems of young trees. They continue growing and producing fruit. These trees and their apples still grow today.

Many states where Chapman planted apple seeds celebrate him. Ohio hosts a Johnny Appleseed Festival. Indiana does too. At this festival, people dress like they would have in the 1800s. They cook over fires.

Johnny Appleseed Day

Johnny Appleseed Day is celebrated on September 26. This was John Chapman's birthday. To celebrate, people can make apple cider. People may sing a song about Johnny Appleseed. Each year there is a celebration in the city where Chapman was born.

They sell food that might have been available when Chapman was alive.

Disney's Appleseed

Legends about Johnny Appleseed have changed over time. Johnny Appleseed is a symbol of American values. He was hardworking, independent, and kind. Over time, details about his life have been **exaggerated**. Some people say that even the most dangerous animals would not harm him, because they knew he would not hurt them. This version of Johnny Appleseed is shown by Walt Disney Productions.

In 1948, Disney released a movie called *Melody Time*. It had several stories, including

In *Melody Time,* Johnny Appleseed becomes friends with all the animals of the forest, including dangerous animals such as a mountain lion.

"The Legend of Johnny Appleseed." The movie shows Johnny Appleseed starting on his journey to plant apple trees. He becomes friends with many animals that follow him on his journey.

A living history event in Indiana in 2017 featured a person dressed as Johnny Appleseed. He taught students about the early United States.

In the movie, Johnny Appleseed plants trees that grow juicy, red apples. Settlers eat these apples. People bake them into pies and pastries.

These were not the bitter apples Chapman really planted.

In stories like Disney's, many parts of John Chapman's life became exaggerated. People sometimes forgot about the real man behind the myth. But John Chapman was real. He is an important part of American history.

Further Evidence

Look at the website below. Does it give any new evidence to support Chapter Three?

Our Johnny Appleseed Tree

abdocorelibrary.com/johnny-appleseed

Legendary Facts

Johnny Appleseed is more than a legend. He was a real man named John Chapman.

Johnny Appleseed is known for walking barefoot and wearing a tin pan as a hat. He carried a leather sack full of seeds.

John Chapman traveled across the United States planting apple seeds.

Johnny Appleseed never hurt other living things. Some stories say that wild animals even followed him around.

Glossary

bacteria
tiny living things that can sometimes cause disease

exaggerated
became more dramatic or larger than life

generous
characterized by kindness and the giving of money or other valuable materials to others

legend
a famous story of the past that is not always true

orchards
areas of land where many fruit trees are planted

settlers
people who move to live in an area that is new to them

Online Resources

To learn more about Johnny Appleseed, visit our free resource websites below.

Core Library CONNECTION
FREE! COMMON CORE MULTIMEDIA RESOURCES

Visit **abdocorelibrary.com** or scan this QR code for free Common Core resources for teachers and students, including vetted activities, multimedia, and booklinks, for deeper subject comprehension.

Booklinks NONFICTION NETWORK
FREE! ONLINE NONFICTION RESOURCES

Visit **abdobooklinks.com** or scan this QR code for free additional online weblinks for further learning. These links are routinely monitored and updated to provide the most current information available.

Learn More

Hudak, Heather C. *Paul Bunyan and Babe the Blue Ox.* Abdo, 2024.

Murray, Julie. *Ohio.* Abdo, 2020.

Richmond, Marley. *Pecos Bill.* Abdo, 2024.

Index

animals, 9, 24–25
apple cider, 16–17, 21, 23
apple seeds, 6–7, 9, 11, 15, 17, 23

Bible, 14

Chapman, John, 10–11, 13–18, 19, 21–24, 27
Congress, US, 15

festivals, 23

grafting, 17, 22–23

Johnny Appleseed Day, 23

Leominster, Massachusetts, 13

Melody Time, 24–27

Northwest Territory, 11, 15, 18

Prohibition Era, 21

settlers, 10, 14–15, 17–18, 26
shoes, 7
Swedenborg, Emanuel, 14

About the Author

Marley Richmond is a children's book editor and author. She lives in Minnesota with her cat, Bean.